T0084310

Fun and Games with the Recorder

by Gudrun Heyens and Gerhard Engel
Translated and adapted by Peter Bowman

Method for the Alto Recorder

Alto recorder with other instruments
(S, A, T, B, recorders; piano; guitar and percussion ad. lib.)

With illustrations by John Minnion

Tune book **1**
ED 12704

www.schott-music.com

Mainz · London · Madrid · New York · Paris · Prague · Tokyo · Toronto
© 1998 SCHOTT MUSIK INTERNATIONAL GmbH & Co. KG, Mainz · English translation/adaption © 2004 Schott & Co. Ltd, London · Printed in Germany

Contents

ED 12704

British Library Cataloguing-in-Publication Data.
A catalogue record for this book is available from the British Library.

ISMN M-2201-2258-3
ISBN 1-902455-14-2

© 1998 Schott Musik International GmbH & Co. KG, Mainz
English translation/adaption © 2004 Schott & Co. Ltd, London

Cover illustration John Minnion
Text illustrations Julie Beech, John Minnion
Design Peter Klein
Music setting Jack Thomson

Printed in Germany · S&Co. 7433

1 **Ode to Joy**

Ludwig van Beethoven

2 **Three Duets**

G. Engel

© 2004 Schott & Co. Ltd, London

3

G. Heyens

4

G. Heyens

© 2004 Schott & Co. Ltd, London

5   Oh, When the Saints

Spiritual
Setting: Fritz Emonts

Oh, when the Saints _____ go march - ing in, _____ oh, when the
Saints go march - ing in, _____ then Lord let me be in that
num - ber _____ oh, when the Saints go march - ing in. _____

© 2004 Schott & Co. Ltd, London

6   Winter Goodbye

German traditional
Setting: Johannes Runge

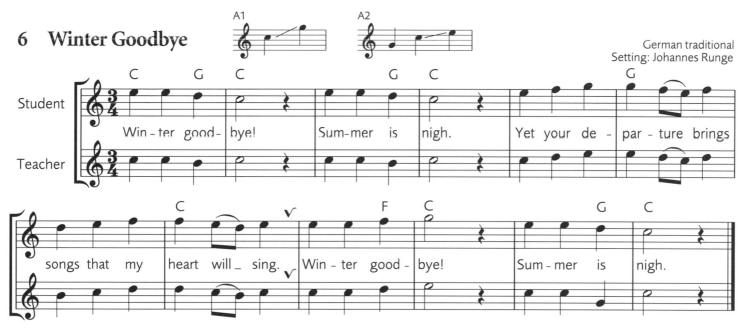

Student

Teacher

Win - ter good - bye! Sum - mer is nigh. Yet your de - par - ture brings
songs that my heart will _ sing. Win - ter good - bye! Sum - mer is nigh.

© 2004 Schott & Co. Ltd, London

7   Cuckoo, Cuckoo

German Folk song
Words: P. C. B.
Setting: J. Runge

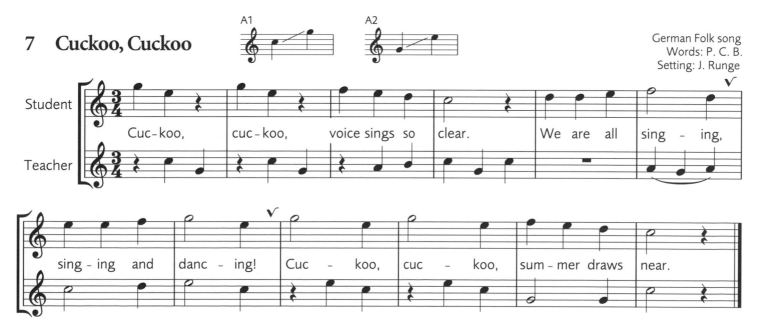

Student

Teacher

Cuc - koo, cuc - koo, voice sings so clear. We are all sing - ing,
sing - ing and danc - ing! Cuc - koo, cuc - koo, sum - mer draws near.

From: *Lied und Tanz. Volkslieder und Volkstänze für 2 Altblockflöten*, Schott ED 4362

8   Hurray, It's Summer Time Again

Setting: J. Runge
Text: P. C. B.

Hey, hur – ray, it's sum – mer time a – gain. We'll

play out in the gar – den, with joy and cel – e – bra – tion.

Hey, hur – ray, it's sum – mer time a – gain.

© 2004 Schott & Co. Ltd, London

9   Summer's Birds Are Back Again

© 2004 Schott & Co. Ltd, London

10 Engels Lied

Jacob van Eyck
(1590–1657)
Setting: G. Heyens

© 2004 Schott & Co. Ltd, London

11 Hark, There's Someone Passing By

German Folk song

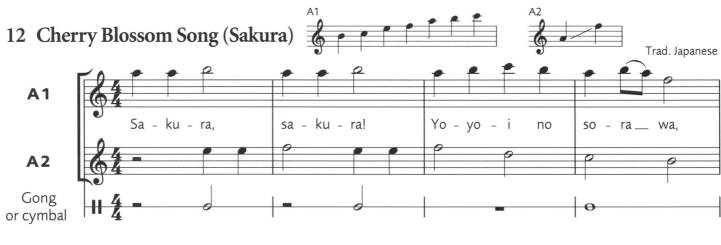

© 2004 Schott & Co. Ltd, London

12 Cherry Blossom Song (Sakura)

Trad. Japanese

Sa - ku - ra, sa - ku - ra! Yo - yo - i no so - ra __ wa,

mi - va - ta - su ka - ghi - ri. Ka - su - mi - ka? ku - mo _ ka? Ni - o - i zo

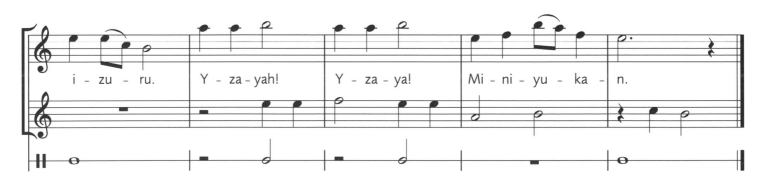

i - zu - ru. Y - za - yah! Y - za - ya! Mi - ni - yu - ka - n.

Translation:
Cherry tree, cherry tree your blossom shines so bright
I seek the shade of a tree. Your perfume floats in the air like the clouds in the sky.
Cherry tree, cherry tree, pretty cherry tree.

© 2004 Schott & Co. Ltd, London

13 Come, You Play Fellows

German Folk song

© 2004 Schott & Co. Ltd, London

14 Nobody Knows

Spiritual
Setting: Hans-Martin Linde

No - bod - y knows the trou - ble I've seen. No - bod - y knows but

Je - sus;_____ No - bod - y knows the trou - ble I've seen,

Glor - y hal - le - lu - ja. Some - times I'm up, some - times I'm down,

oh, yes Lord! Some - times I'm al - most to the ground, oh, yes Lord! Oh,

© 2004 Schott & Co. Ltd, London

15 Dance With Me

V. Haussmann
(ca. 1600)
Arr: E. Reichelt

From: *Bach to Hassler, Easy Recorder Quartets*, Schott ED 7819

10

16 Motet (Ben Venga Maggio)

Anon.
(ca. 1480)

© 2004 Schott & Co. Ltd, London

17 Drinking Song

H. Finck
(ca. 1445–1527)

From: *The Recorder Consort Anthology*, Vol. 5, German and Dutch Music, Schott ED 12391

18 The Farmer in Spring

Czech Folk song

© 2004 Schott & Co. Ltd, London

19 Minuet

Valentin Rathgeber
(1682–1750)

FINE

D. C. al Fine

From: Kleine Duette alter Meister, Schott ED 4373

20 London Bridge

Setting: W. Drahts

© 2004 Schott & Co. Ltd, London

21 Syncopation Duet

G. Heyens

FINE

D. C. al Fine

© 2004 Schott & Co. Ltd, London

22 Morning Walk

Alexander Gretchaninoff
(1864–1956)
op. 126b

© 2004 Schott & Co. Ltd, London

23 Red River Valley

from America

A

From this val – ley they say you are go – ing,_____ I will miss your bright eyes and sweet smile: _____ for they say you are tak – ing the sun – shine _____ that _ bright – ens our path – way a while. _____

© 2004 Schott & Co. Ltd, London

24 Bassedance "Bernadine"

Jean d'Estrées
(d. 1756)

S1

S2

A

T

From: *The Recorder Consort Anthology*, Vol. 4, Dance Music, Schott ED 12390

17

25 Spring is Here

Folk song
Setting: R. Mohrs

© 2004 Schott & Co. Ltd, London

26 Travellers Arise

Folk song
Setting: G.H.

© 2004 Schott & Co. Ltd, London

Fun and Games with the Recorder

by Gudrun Heyens and Gerhard Engel
Translated and adapted by Peter Bowman

Method for the Alto Recorder

Tune book **1**
Piano Part

ED 12704

www.schott-music.com

Mainz · London · Madrid · New York · Paris · Prague · Tokyo · Toronto
© 1998 SCHOTT MUSIK INTERNATIONAL GmbH & Co. KG, Mainz · English translation/adaption © 2004 Schott & Co. Ltd, London · Printed in Germany

1 Ode to Joy

Ludwig van Beethoven

© 2004 Schott & Co. Ltd, London

5 Oh, When the Saints

Spiritual
Setting: Fritz Emonts

Oh, when the Saints _____ go march-ing in, _____ oh, when the

Saints go march - ing in, _____ then Lord let me be in that

© 2004 Schott & Co. Ltd, London

num – ber _____ oh, when the Saints go march – ing in. _____

11 Hark, There's Someone Passing By

German Folk song

© 2004 Schott & Co. Ltd, London

14 Nobody Knows

Spiritual
Setting: Hans-Martin Linde

No-bod - y knows the trou-ble I've seen. No-bod - y knows but

Je - sus; _____ No-bod - y knows the trou-ble I've seen,

Glor - y hal - le - lu - ja. Some-times I'm up, some-times I'm down,

oh, yes Lord! Some-times I'm al-most to the ground, oh, yes Lord! Oh,

© 2004 Schott & Co. Ltd, London

22 Morning Walk

Alexander Gretchaninoff
(1864–1956)
op. 126b

© 2004 Schott & Co. Ltd, London

23 Red River Valley

from America
Setting: Rainer Mohrs

From this val - ley they say you are go - ing, _____ I will

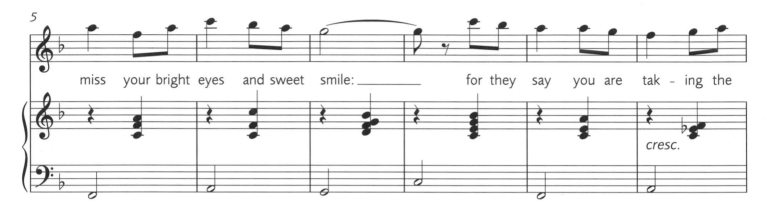

miss your bright eyes and sweet smile: _____ for they say you are tak - ing the

sun - shine _____ that _ bright - ens our path - way a while. _____

© 2004 Schott & Co. Ltd, London

25 Spring is Here

Folk song
Setting: R. Mohrs

© 2004 Schott & Co. Ltd, London

6

27 Wanderer's Song

Folk song
Setting: G. H.

© 2004 Schott & Co. Ltd, London

28 Korean Song

Setting: Lin Jong-Teh

© 2004 Schott & Co. Ltd, London

36 The Poacher

Setting: Freda Dinn

From: Freda Dinn, *My Recorder Tune Book*, Schott ED 10077-01

38 Contredance No. 1

J. B. de Boismortier
(1689–1755)
Piano setting: G. H.

© 2004 Schott & Co. Ltd, London

40 The Rising of the Lark

Freda Dinn

From: Freda Dinn, *My Recorder Tune Book*, Schott ED 10077-01

Contents

27 Wanderer's Song

Folk song
Setting: G. H.

© 2004 Schott & Co. Ltd, London

28 Korean Song

Setting: Lin Jong-Teh

© 2004 Schott & Co. Ltd, London

29 Cai, Cai, Balão

from Brazil
Setting: W. Drahts

© 2004 Schott & Co. Ltd, London

30 The Fireman

F. J. Giesbert

© 2004 Schott & Co. Ltd, London

31 The Night Watch

Folk song
Setting: G. H.

© 2004 Schott & Co. Ltd, London

32 The Post

Folk song
Setting: F. J. Giesbert

© 2004 Schott & Co. Ltd, London

33 Miner's Song

Setting: G. H.

(Teacher)

© 2004 Schott & Co. Ltd, London

34 Polonaise

Anon.

© 2004 Schott & Co. Ltd, London

35 Sarabande

Anon.

© 2004 Schott & Co. Ltd, London

36 The Poacher

Setting: Freda Dinn

From: Freda Dinn, *My Recorder Tune Book*, Schott ED 10077-01

37 Oh, Susanna

from America
Setting: W. Drahts

© 2004 Schott & Co. Ltd, London

1-37b

Claves

Hand Drum

1-37c

Bass Instrument

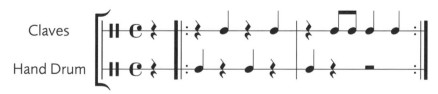

38 Two Contredances
No. 1

J. B. de Boismortier
(1689–1755)
Piano setting: G. H.

© 2004 Schott & Co. Ltd, London

No. 2

J. B. de Boismortier
Tenor part: G. H.

repeat Contre dance No. 1

© 2004 Schott & Co. Ltd, London

27

40 The Rising of the Lark

Freda Dinn

From: Freda Dinn, *My Recorder Tune Book*, Schott ED 10077-01

41 Bicinia 1

Bernado Lupacchino
(ca. 1550)

*) Original = E♭

29

42 Bicinia 2

Bernado Lupacchino
(ca. 1550)

From: *Bicinien for 2 Violins (flutes)*, Ed. Doflein, Schott ED 2208

Bird Song

43 First Tune for the Bullfinch

44 Second Tune for the Bullfinch

45 Tune for the Canary Bird

From: *The Bird Fancyer's Delight*, Schott ED 10442

About the composers

Ludwig van Beethoven
Born 1770 in Bonn, Germany
Died 1827 in Vienna, Austria

Ludwig van Beethoven was one of the most important composers of the classical period. He was born into a poor family and his father, who brought him up very strictly, was a singer in the service of the Elector of Cologne at Bonn. He gave his first musical performance at the age of eight and at thirteen was a member of the court orchestra. Because his father was an alcoholic Ludwig had to leave school early to look after his family. However, he worked very hard and soon got to know the most important musicians of his time. In 1792 Beethoven moved to live in Vienna which at that time was one of the most famous musical centres in Europe. Because he did not have a permanent position at court he had to make his living from giving concerts and above all from composing. Apart from that, he had many noble friends to whom he dedicated his works.

From around 1800 Beethoven began suffering from the hearing problems which would eventually leave him totally deaf so that he never heard his last works. As a person Beethoven was a difficult character and often argued with his friends and colleagues. Although he was deaf he composed some of the greatest works of music during his last years. As well as 32 piano sonatas, a violin concerto, numerous other solo concertos and 16 string quartets, his nine symphonies and his only opera, "Fidelio", are his most important works.

Joseph-Bodin de Boismortier
Born 1689 in Thionville, eastern France
Died 1755 in Roissy-en-Brie, near Paris

Joseph-Bodin de Boismortier lived during the baroque period at roughly the same time as Johann Sebastian Bach. He never left France and was most famous there as a composer of opera-ballets. Apart from that he was a prolific composer who made a large amount of money writing all kinds of instrumental music including numerous pieces for recorder.

Jean d'Estrée
Date of birth unknown
Died 1576 in Paris

Jean d'Estrée was an oboist and a member of the "Musique du Roi" (The King's Music) in Paris. d'Estrée is best known for his four-volume collection of dances for 4 instruments.

Jacob van Eyck
Born around 1590 in Holland
Died 1657 in Utrecht

Although van Eyck was mainly a carillonneur who was also responsible for the care and maintenance of the church bells in Utrecht, he is in fact one of the most important Dutch composers of the 17th century. All recorder players will eventually come across the works of Jacob van Eyck because he composed the "Fluyten Lusthof", a three-volume work consisting of 167 pieces for one or two recorders. Van Eyck was above all a master of improvisation.

Heinrich Finck

Born around 1445 in Bamberg, Germany
Died 1527 in Vienna, Austria

Heinrich Finck only began to study music when he was 38 years old and from 1492 worked as a choir master at courts in Poland. He later became orchestra leader at larger courts such as Salzburg and Vienna. He composed sacred and secular songs as well as masses and motets.

Alexander Gretchaninof

Born 1864 in Moscow, Russia
Died 1956 in New York

The Russian composer Alexander Gretchaninof was a student of Rimski-Korsakov. From 1925 he lived in Paris and later moved to America. As well as five symphonies and four string quartets he composed over 250 songs and duets. He became well known for his easy and attractive compositions for children.

Valentin Haussmann

Date of birth unknown
Died 1611 in Gerbstätt (Germany)

Valentin Haussmann came from a famous family of organists and wrote a large amount of dance music and other instrumental pieces.

Bernado Lupacchino

Bernado Lupacchino was a musician and composer who lived and worked in Italy during the 16th century. The exact dates of his birth and death are unknown. From 1552 he was orchestra leader in Rome and was a predecessor of Giovanni Palestrina at the church of St. John Lateran there. However, because of his poor lifestyle he had to give up the post after three years. Lupacchino wrote numerous madrigals and bicinias.

Valentin Rathgeber

Born 1682 in Oberelsbach
Died 1750 Banz

Valentin Rathgeber was born the son of a village school teacher. His father gave him his first music lessons and he later studied rhetoric, mathematics, law and finally theology at the university in Würzburg. At the age of 25 he entered the service of the Abbot at the benedictine monastery in Banz as a musician and 5 years later was invested as a priest. He served at the monastery as 'cellist, gambist, organist and composer of instrumental and small scale choral works. Against the wishes of the Abbot he undertook a 9 year long study tour of the German-speaking countries in order to learn more about music and the latest musical styles. On his return to the monastery he was imprisoned for a short time as punishment but was soon allowed to return to his post as musician where he lived peacefully until his death at the age of 68.

About the Pieces

Bassedance p.16

A serious and highly formalised ancient processional dance for couples, originally with three beats in a measure, later with two beats per measure and in some cases with a mixture of the two as in this *bassedance* by Jean d'Estrée.

Bicinia p. 29 – 30

Bicinias are two-part pieces for voices or instruments. They were popular during the 15th – 17th and even into the 18th century and were used mainly for study purposes. Bicinia have been taken up again by composers in our own time (Bartók, Hindemith).

Contredance p. 26 – 27

This duple time dance, known in France as "contredanse" (from English, "country dance"), was a favourite at the French court during the 18th century. Danced as either a line-dance for couples or in a larger group, the contredance was as popular as the minuet.

Polonaise p. 22

The Polonaise, originally a processional dance in duple time, was often followed by an after-dance in triple time. The pair of contrasting dances originated in Poland where they are still performed to open ceremonies and festivals. Since the 17th century the polonaise has also existed as a purely instrumental piece.

Motet p. 11

A motet is a polyphonic song for choir which has its origins in the Roman Catholic church service. Motets were also played by instrumentalists as a kind of 'song without words'. Polyphonic describes music with a number of independent voices or parts.

Sarabande p. 23

The sarabande is a dance of Spanish origin which was widely known during the 17th and 18th centuries. Sarabandes also exist as pure instrumental music. Sources from the 16th century tell us that it was a wild and exotic dance. During the 17th century, however, the tempo slowed down except in England where it continued to exist in the fast form. Sarabandes are usually in a calm 3/2 or 3/4 time and as well as a strong first beat the dotted rhythm adds an extra stress to the second beat:

Spiritual p. 5, p. 9

The spiritual is a religious song of the American negros which often lasts for hours and is accompanied by clapping and stamping. The song is often repeated with added improvisations and decorations.

Syncopation p. 14

Syncopation is when the normal accent of a rhythm is moved from the strong beat to a weak beat.

FUN AND GAMES with the RECORDER

A special method for beginners

Three volumes for the descant recorder which advance in small steps and include many playful elements suitable for both group and individual lessons.

- Discover the adventure of learning the recorder
- Make real progress through games: breathing, articulation, rhythm, tone
- A mixture of lively new and traditional tunes
- Three supplementary tune books each with a sheet of stickers
- Teacher's commentary
- Join Dotty-do-a-lot and her friends in the exciting world of music

Tutor Book 1	ED 12590	Tune Book 1	ED 12591
Tutor Book 2	ED 12592	Tune Book 2	ED 12593
Tutor Book 3	ED 12594	Tune Book 3	ED 12595

Teacher's Commentary	ED 12596
Dotty's Notebook	ED 12641

♪ SCHOTT

48 Great Marlborough Street, London W1F 7BB. Tel: +44 (0)20 7437 1246 Fax: +44 (0)20 7437 6115
Email: marketing@schott-music.com Website: www.schott-music.com

---

NEW PLAY-ALONG RECORDER MUSIC FROM SCHOTT

Folksongs
for treble recorder (includes optional second part)
edited by Hans and Marianne Magolt
A modern collection of folk pieces in very easy arrangements, the accompaniment on CD helps with practice and makes lessons more enjoyable.
Contents: Alas My Love (Greensleeves) - Morning Has Broken - I've Been A Wild Rover - Auld Lang Syne - Amazing Grace - Kalinka - Casatschok - Bella Bimba - Tiritomba - Il Etait Un Petit Navire - Plaisir d'amour - Cielito Lindo - La Cucaracha - La Paloma - Andean Melody - Oh Happy Day - Swing Low - Yankee Doodle - Tom Dooley
ED 9531-01
Book and CD

Classic Hits
for soprano/descant recorder (includes optional second part)
edited by Hans Magolt and Rainer Buts
A volume of popular classical melodies in easy arrangements.
Now recorder players can play the catchiest classical hits with an orchestral accompaniment on CD.
Contents include:
'Ode to Joy' (Beethoven) - 'Eine kleine Nachtmusik' (Mozart) - 'The Moldau' (Smetana) - the Birdcatcher's Song (Mozart) - Toreador (Bizet) - 'La donna é mobile' (Verdi) - Barcarole (Offenbach) and numerous other well-known melodies.
ED 9576-01
Book and CD

♪ SCHOTT

48 Great Marlborough Street, London W1F 7BB. Tel: +44 (0)20 7437 1246 Fax: +44 (0)20 7437 6115
Email: marketing@schott-music.com Website: www.schott-music.com

RECORDER MUSIC BY BRIAN BONSOR FROM SCHOTT

The astonishing popularity of the works of Brian Bonsor derives from his declared aim to provide attractive and effective concert pieces at all technical levels, always with interesting and tuneful parts that will extend players' technique and musicianship.

Simple Samba
for two descant recorders or descant/treble and Piano
This easy and attractive concert piece is dedicated 'to those who asked for an easier part'
Grade 2
ED 11422

Rumba
Exhilarating, demanding precise rhythm and neat articulation.
Grade 3
ED 10698

The Easy Winners
for descant, treble and piano
(Joplin, S. arr. Bonsor)
A highly effective and technically demanding setting of a Joplin piano rag.
'Not easy - but a winner.'
(The Recorder)
Grade 3-4
ED 12202

Beguine
Though technically easy (descants D-E' with C sharp), extended passages in unison and octaves demand careful tuning.
Grade 2-3
ED 10700

SCHOTT

48 Great Marlborough Street, London W1F 7BB. Tel: +44 (0)20 7437 1246 Fax: +44 (0)20 7437 6115
Email: marketing@schott-music.com Website: www.schott-music.com

NEW RECORDER MUSIC FROM SCHOTT

The Horns of Elfland
by Markus Zahnhausen, for solo tenor recorder based upon a poem by Alfred, Lord Tennyson. 'The Horns of Elfland' received its UK premiere at the ERTA (UK) conference in June 2000 and is a fascinating addition to the solo repertoire.
OFB 198

Miniatures
by Harald Genzmer, for 3 recorders (SAT) edited by Gudrun Heyens.
Contents: Moderato - Fugue - Tarantella - Trouvère's song with two variations - Intermezzo - Amabile - Giocoso - Irish Song

These eight easy pieces for recorder trio offer a delightful blend of the old and the new, suitable for tuition and concert performance.
OFB 200

Reminiscences
by Hans-Martin Linde, for Recorder Quartet (ATTB). Reminiscences uses musical themes from the 15th to 17th Centuries: a 'Prélude à l'imitation' by Froberger, a melody by Claudio Saraceni 'Da te parto', themes from keyboard sonatas by Domenico Scarlatti, the Chanson 'Adieu, mes très belles' by Binchois and a ground bass from Purcell's harpsichord collection 'Musik's Handmaid'.
OFB 202

SCHOTT

48 Great Marlborough Street, London W1F 7BB. Tel: +44 (0)20 7437 1246 Fax: +44 (0)20 7437 6115
Email: marketing@schott-music.com Website: www.schott-music.com